P9-DBI-481

FRANK LLOYD WRIGHT

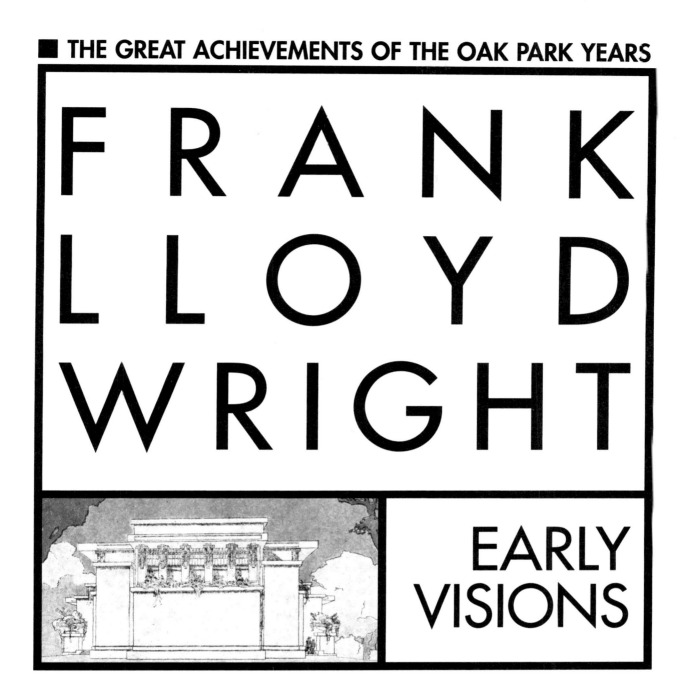

EARLY VISIONS

■ THE GREAT ACHIEVEMENTS OF THE OAK PARK YEARS

FRANK LLOYD WRIGHT

EARLY VISIONS

THE COMPLETE *FRANK LLOYD WRIGHT: AUSGEFUHRTE BAUTEN* OF 1911,
SUPPLEMENTED BY ADDITIONAL ILLUSTRATIONS FROM
FRANK LLOYD WRIGHT: CHICAGO, 1911

**With a New Foreword by Nancy Frazier
English Translations by Brigitte Goldstein**

GRAMERCY BOOKS
New York ■ Avenel

720.92
WRI

ABOUT THIS EDITION

This Gramercy edition is an unabridged reproduction of the *Ausgefuhrte Bauten,* a collection of photographs of architecture by Frank Lloyd Wright that was first published in Berlin by Ernst Wasmuth in 1911. C. R. Ashbee's introduction and all of the captions have been newly translated from the original German for this edition. A German-English glossary of terms found in the ground plans is also included. Another unique feature of this Gramercy edition is a special section containing material from a second Wasmuth version of the 1911 book. The selections from *Frank Lloyd Wright: Chicago* (Number 8 of the series *Sonderheft der Architektur des XX Jahrhunderts*) are reproductions of all the photographs from this alternate version that did not appear in the *Ausgefuhrte Bauten.*

Frontispiece: Avery Coonley house, Riverside, Illinois (1908).

Foreword, English translations, and compilation
copyright © 1995 by Random House Value Publishing, Inc.
All rights reserved.

This edition is published by Gramercy Books,
distributed by Random House Value Publishing, Inc.,
40 Engelhard Avenue, Avenel, New Jersey 07001.

Printed and bound in the United States of America

Library of Congress Cataloging-in-Publication Data
Wright, Frank Lloyd, 1867–1959.
      Frank Lloyd Wright: early visions.
             p. cm.
      Introduction, compilation, and new English translation — T.p. verso.
      ISBN 0-517-14722-X
      1. Wright, Frank Lloyd, 1867–1959 — Themes, motives. 2. Prairie school
(Architecture) — Illinois — Oak Park. 3. Prairie school (Architecture) — Illinois — Chicago.
4. Oak Park (Ill.) — Buildings, structures, etc. 5. Chicago (Ill.) — Buildings, structures, etc.
I. Title
NA737.W7A4 1995
720'.92—dc20
                                      95-18268
                                          CIP

8 7 6 5 4 3 2 1

35,00

■ CONTENTS

FRANK LLOYD WRIGHT'S CHICAGO STUDIO.

■ FOREWORD

AFTER TRAVELING seventy-eight thousand miles to see all the buildings designed by Frank Lloyd Wright that were still standing in the 1970s, an architectural historian commented that it was "like having heard every work of Beethoven, not just the masterpieces." Now, comparing Wright to a German composer might be considered inappropriate, since Wright was the most resolutely American of American architects. In an era when his colleagues looked, and often went, to the great European centers for ideas and training, Wright stayed home and worked on inventing a proudly national style. However, Ludwig van Beethoven was arguably the greatest composer in history, his music above and beyond constrictions of time and place. Frank Lloyd Wright was similarly outside such delimitation. And, it might be added, he used to tell his students that if he were a musician, he would be as great as Beethoven.

This book, first published as *Ausgefuhrte Bauten* in Germany in 1911, reveals Wright's genius as it first took hold and developed. Here are the works of what is called his Oak Park period, the time between 1893 and 1910 when Wright lived and worked in Oak Park, Illinois. Included are more than thirty houses, although very few public buildings. Interestingly, the most notable of the public places, Unity Temple and the Larkin building, come first and last among the photographs. Why they are arranged in this order is not explained — the flow of the book is not essentially chronological. But perhaps we may infer a philosophical meaning: Unity Temple is a place of worship, the Larkin building a place of work, and the homes between them are places that enclose family and personal values, where profession and religion meet in people's daily lives.

This implies a deep well of moral values, and Wright was as insistently a moralist as he was a patriot. A careful observer of the photographs in this volume notices homilies in unexpected places: the wall of Browne's bookstore in Chicago, above the fireplace in the Heath house in Buffalo, in Wright's own studio — a marvelous army of good, uplifting words, all carrying the implied codes of the highest standards of behavior. These rules were proclaimed on the interior balustrades and outside walls of the Larkin building. For example: *Intelligence . . . Enthusiasm . . . Control* are values to inspire the workers, and *Honest Labor Needs No Slaves* on the facade greeted them as they arrived for a day's work, and sent them home at the end of the day. Although not visible in this volume, there is an inscription over the west patio entrance of Unity Temple that proclaims the building's dedication: *For the Worship of God and the Service of Man.* Such were the architect's concise sermons engraved in stone.

Wright's morality was overarching, but not within conventional mandates. In 1909, at the age of forty-two, he walked out on his wife and children. He had fallen in love with a client's wife. To the public, especially at that time when divorce and scandal were synonymous, his action was reprehensible. He argued it was a virtuous decision, that he was following the truth of his love, his soul, and even God. Wright left his Oak Park practice, and he and his beloved mistress, Mamah Borthwick Cheney, ran away to Europe.

This flight was not entirely an amorous escape. Wright had business to do in Germany. Although his practice was prospering in Illinois, his reputation was modest in the United States. As his earlier employer and mentor Louis Sullivan had learned, Americans were not ready to approve, let alone applaud, an indigenous architecture. The monumental World's Columbian Exposition of 1893 in Chicago had proved that the aesthetic of the Beaux Arts school of architecture, using columns and pediments on buildings that resembled Greek temples, was still the standard. Despite Sullivan's and, later, Wright's protestations, Americans did not yet trust themselves to break away from the European canon.

In Europe, however, Sullivan and Wright were appreciated. In fact, Wright was so highly esteemed that publication of his works was being assembled in Germany. When Wright and Cheney left for Europe together, Wright went to Berlin in order to oversee the major monographs being prepared by Ernst Wasmuth. In 1910 Wasmuth first published the

Ausgefuhrte Bauten und Entwurfe, a gorgeous portfolio containing one hundred plates in unbound sheets. These showed both architectural plans and details of the ornaments on Wright's most important buildings to date. It has been called the greatest architectural publication of the twentieth century, and it represented the epitome of modern architecture for decades, if not right up to the postmodern era. The following year Wasmuth published *Frank Lloyd Wright: Ausgefuhrte Bauten,* of which this book is a facsimile. It is popularly known as the little Wasmuth to distinguish it from the portfolio and is the first published collection of photographs of Wright's work. The introduction by C. R. Ashbee was translated into German; Wright visited the Arts and Crafts leader in England in 1910 and asked him to provide it. This book inspired a wider public than the earlier one, since it provided an opportunity for nonprofessionals to see and understand the new kind of architecture that was being made in America.

What exactly was new about all this? To the extent that style represents concept, almost everything. To Sullivan's revolutionary dictum that form must follow function, Wright had added the concept that site and structure must be in harmony. He wanted an organic architecture, a building that seemed part of the earth, that embraced the ground out of which it should seem to grow. Materials were to be natural, as closely related to the site as possible and, also when possible, not painted over.

These were enormous changes, but change is a slower process than we often recognize. The beauty of this book is that we are able to see it taking place. Some of the buildings, like the 1893 Winslow residence in River Forest, remain attached to such earlier conventions as a pitched roof, foursquare walls, and double–hung windows. The Winslow house was Wright's first independent commission after he left the employ of Adler and Sullivan, and its ornamentation is reminiscent of Louis Sullivan's designs. The elaborate tracery of the second story is visible, although the beautiful detailing around the entranceway is less so. The latter contains elongated diamond shapes surrounded by delicate detailing that looks like embroidery in stone. A panel in the wooden door itself is carved with a lacy vegetal arabesque. These are allusions not only to Sullivan, but to Islamic design as well. Significantly, there are signs of Wright's future directions in the firmness with which the house sits on the ground and its overhanging eaves. The architect's growing pride and sense of self are reflected by a unique touch: if you face the side entrance and look down in the lower right corner of the stone base, you will discover a small emblem, a cross inside a circle enclosed within a square. This was Wright's signature, which shows him to be one of the few architects to "sign" their buildings on site. Later he reduced his logo down to the well-known symbol, a red square.

Born in rural Wisconsin — where he would eventually resettle and build Taliesin, his home/studio/school (another Taliesin is in Scottsdale, Arizona) — Wright began his career as an apprentice to Chicago architect Joseph Lyman Silsbee. He next worked as a draftsman for Adler & Sullivan. When the principals were absorbed with large commercial projects, they turned a number of their small, domestic commissions over to Wright. During that same period he was moonlighting on house designs outside of the office, which led to his being fired. But it also led to his developing a successful practice in residential architecture.

Wright's genius was extraordinary and timeless, but his concepts were nevertheless firmly grounded in his era, particularly in the Arts and Crafts movement that flourished in America between 1875 and 1920. A movement of reaction and reform, it grew in both England and the United States. It was a reaction against the degradation and dehumanization brought on by industrialization, which had been growing in strength and velocity throughout the nineteenth century. Industrialization was held responsible for the social ills of poverty, overcrowding, labor unrest, child labor — indeed, for the pervasive fin de siècle malaise. Reform measures were wide ranging. One idea was to return to medieval craft systems; another solution was a retreat to utopian communities, several of which were founded. But the most widespread and enduring concept was to return to the direct, individual, careful production of objects of beauty made by human hands, not by factory machines. While Britain's John Ruskin and William Morris were known as forerunners of the movement, Frank Lloyd Wright would become its most renowned American star. The style of his architecture fit into what was called the Prairie School, and its strongest inspiration was the landscape of the Midwest, the long, horizontal horizon of the western plains.

There are ironic notes to this. First, in 1893, just as the Midwest was coming into its own, Frederick Jackson Turner gave his famous eulogy to the vanishing frontier. The World's Columbian Exposition was being held at the time, and the American Historical Association was also meeting in Chicago when Turner lamented that the pioneer journey through the West, the spirit of adventurers pushing on to the Pacific coast — "the frontier individualism [that] has from the beginning promoted democracy" — had ended. He wrote: "And now, four centuries from the discovery of America, at the end of a hundred years of life under the Constitution, the frontier has gone, and with its going has closed the first period of American history."

While Turner bemoaned the closing of the West, Wright and others were insisting on its viability. The Prairie style is seen in a building such as Unity Temple, in houses such as the Susan Lawrence Dana residence, and in the Frederick C. Robie residence, its most famous and mature expression. The Robie house has been designated a national landmark by the American Institute of Architects — one of the seventeen American buildings by Wright to be preserved for the public. These ground-hugging, horizon-loving, organic-seeming structures were his hallmark. However, it is another irony that the majority of Wright's Prairie-style houses were not located on the prairie at all; rather, they sat on suburban streets, surrounded by houses of very conventional design. A final irony to be noted is that the European architects who contemplated Wright's buildings with such awe really did not understand either their geographic references to the wide-open plains of mid-America or their actual siting in suburban streets. Nevertheless, they admired the revolutionary import of his ideas.

Inside Wright houses, leaded-glass windows, in increasingly simple designs (compared to the ornamental elaboration on the earlier Winslow residence), were tinted in wheat golds and earth browns — colors of the land. These windows remind us of the Gothic notion of Divine Light pouring into a cathedral to bring the harmony of faith and reason to human understanding. And, most astonishing to people accustomed to living in houses rigorously partitioned by walls, Wright opened up the interiors of his buildings. Spaces flowed one into the other, removing boundaries that separated various domestic activities. About the Martin house a European architect wrote:

> The interior affords beautiful views, not only from room to room, but also from rooms into the halls, toward the staircase and so on. . . . I had the impression of an extraordinary intimacy, and only with great effort could I tear myself away from these rooms.

These interior views, it might be added, would reduce the temptation to look out the window at the houses along the street. Why? Wright was not hesitant to expound on his opinion of other designers:

> What was the matter with the typical American house? Well, just for an honest beginning, it lied about everything. It had no sense of unity at all nor any such sense of space as should belong to a free people. It was stuck up in thoughtless fashion. It had no more sense of earth than a "modernistic" house. And it was stuck up on whatever it happened to be. To take any of these so-called "homes" away would have improved the landscape and helped to clear the atmosphere.

Those harsh words were written by Wright in *The Natural House*, published in 1954. It certainly explains part of his determination to direct the gaze inward, rather than out to the street. Moreover, as often as possible, Wright also designed the fixtures and furniture for his houses. The moral rectitude of his homilies is reflected in the stern, sturdy, rectilinear geometry of his chairs and tables and the geometric eloquence of his lighting fixtures. He was offering his clients solace from the crude world of the philistines outside their walls.

The years covered in this book were the idealistic, formative years of Frank Lloyd Wright's career. In many ways, they were the most important years. A number of the buildings reproduced have been demolished, but many others still stand. Indeed, today under the auspices of the National Trust for Historic Preservation, Oak Park celebrates the Frank Lloyd Wright Prairie School of Architecture in a National Historic District, with twenty-five structures by Wright. It is the largest collection of his built designs in the world. His home and studio at 951 Chicago Avenue, where he lived and worked from 1889 to 1909, is open to the public, and tours of his other buildings may by arranged. The spirit of these early works, which can be seen in their natural settings, is still bold and vital — and as uplifting as the greatest, most inspiring symphony.

NANCY FRAZIER

University of Massachusetts,
Amherst, 1995

GLOSSARY OF GERMAN WORDS IN THE GROUND PLANS

Ab. Down.
Abhang. Slope.
Absatz. Landing.
Abzug. Sink.
Alkoven. Alcoves.
Angestellte. Employees.
Ankleidezimmer. Dressing room.
Anrichtezimmer. Pantry.
Arbeitszimmer. Study.
Atelier. Studio.
Auf. Up.
Aufbewahrungsort. Storage room.
Ausgang. Exit.
Bach. Brook.
Bächlein. Rivulet.
Bad. Bath, bathroom.
Balkon. Balcony.
Balkongeschoss[es]. Balcony floor.
Bedeckt[er]. Covered.
Bedeckte Laube. Pergola.
Bedientenzimmer. Servants' quarters.
Bibliothek. Library.
Billiardzimmer. Billiard room.
Blumen. Flowers.
Blumengarten. Flower garden.
Bowling Spielplatz. Bowling alley.
Brücke. Bridge.
Bücher. Books, bookcase.
Bureau, Büro. Office.
Cassirer, Kassierer. Cashier.
Chor. Choir.
Closet, Klosett. Lavatory.
Coje, Koje. Stand, stall.
Corridor, Korridor. Corridor.
Dach. Roof.
Dachgarten. Roof garden.
Deckfenster. Skylight.
Diener. Servant.
Dienerin. Maid.
Dienerinzimmer. Maid's room.
Diensthof. Servants' yard.
Druckerei. Print room.
Eigenes Zimmer. Owner's room.
Eintritts Halle. Entrance hall.
Eis. Ice.
Eltern. Parents.
Empfangszimmer. Reception room.
Entwurfszimmer. Drafting room.
Erdgeschoss[es]. Ground floor.
Erhaben[er]. Raised.
Exhedra. Exedra.

Fahreintritt. Drive entrance.
Fahrräder. Bicycles.
Fahrstuhl. Elevator.
Fahrweg. Driveway.
Feuerfest[es]. Fireproof.
Feuerraum. Furnace room.
Frauen. Ladies.
Frühstück. Breakfast, breakfast room.
Fundament. Basement.
Futter Raum. Feed room.
Galerie. Gallery, hallway.
Garderobe. Checkroom, wardrobe.
Garten. Garden.
Gärtnerhäuschen. Gardener's cottage.
Gast Schlafzimmer. Guest bedroom.
Gastzimmer. Guestroom.
Gehege. Enclosure, pen.
Gewölbe. Vaulted area.
Grundriss. Ground plan.
Halbgrundriss. Half ground plan.
Halbkreiss. Semicircle.
Halle. Hall.
Hauptgeschoss[es]. Main floor.
Haus. House.
Hausmeister. Caretaker.
Heizkörper. Radiator.
Herrenzimmer. Master [bed]room.
Hinter. Rear.
Hof. Court, yard.
Höherer Teil. Upper section.
Hörsaal. Auditorium.
Hühner. Chickens.
Im Freien. Outdoor.
In, im. In.
Kanzel. Pulpit.
Keller. Cellar, basement.
Kinder. Children.
Kinderstube. Nursery.
Klavier. Piano.
Kleider. Clothes, clothes closet.
Kloster. Cloister.
Küche. Kitchen.
Kühlraum. Refrigeration room.
Kuhst, Kuhstall. Cowshed.
Kutschen. Carriages.
Lageplan. Site plan.
Leinen. Linen, linen closet.
Licht. Light.
Lichtschacht. Light well.
Loggia. Loggia, sunroom.
Mädchen. Maid.

Männer. Men.
Möbel. Furniture.
Musik. Music, music room.
Nahstube. Sewing room.
Ober. Upper.
Oberlight. Skylight, ceiling light.
Offen. Open.
Orgel. Organ.
Orgelzimmer. Organ loft.
Pavillon. Pavilion.
Pfarrer. Pastor.
Porte cochere. Roofed driveway.
Rasenplatz. Lawn.
Raum. Room.
Schlafzimmer. Bedroom.
Schrag. Sloped, slanted.
Schrank. Closet.
Schrankzimmer. Locker room, walk–in closet.
Sitz. Seat.
Sitzkasten. Window seat, settle.
Sonntagschule. Sunday school.
Speise Tisch. Dining room.
Stall Hof. Stable yard.
Stall. Stable, stall.
Strasse. Street.
Teich. Pool.
Telefon. Telephone.
Telefonzelle. Telephone booth.
Terrasse. Terrace.
Tisch. Table.
Toiletten. Toilets, bathrooms, powder rooms.
Treppe. Stairway, steps.
Typisch[en]. Typical.
Unterhaltung. Maintenance room.
Versenkt[er]. Sunken.
Vestibul. Vestibule.
Viertelgrundriss. Quarter ground plan.
Vorbau. Porch, pergola.
Vorfahrt. Driveway.
Vorrat. Stock, supply, storeroom.
Vorzimmer. Anteroom.
Wäscherei. Laundry room.
Waschraum. Toilet, bathroom, powder room.
Weg. Pathway, walkway.
Werkstatt. Workshop.
Wohnung. House, apartment, residence.
Wohnungs Saal. Reception room, drawing room.
Wohnzimmer. Living room.
Zimmer. Room.
Zu, zum, zur. To.
Zwischenstock[es]. Mezzanine.

FRANK LLOYD WRIGHT

AUSGEFUHRTE BAUTEN

Originally published by Wasmuth, Berlin, 1911

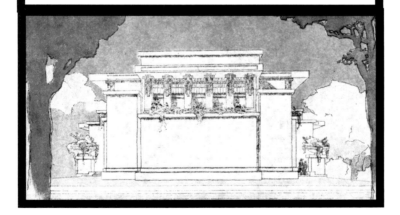

UNITY TEMPLE UNDER CONSTRUCTION, 1908.

2

UNITY TEMPLE MODEL.

FRANK LLOYD WRIGHT
A STUDY OF HIS WORK BY C. R. ASHBEE

AMERICAN ARCHITECTURE plays a prominent role in the development of modern art. Few cities on the vast American continent do not offer architectural landmarks or at least promising endeavors. This has its origin in the American's intrinsic love of architecture. We see men blessed with good fortune openly displaying their wealth in the form of great edifices; we see cities competing with each other in building great libraries, clubs, schools, and universities. Even between the states of the Union the competitive spirit is expressed in the splendor of their statehouses.

Yes, even in circles in which in our country [England] the architect is a rare guest, in America the breath of his spirit can be felt in office and business buildings that have been raised to objects of his art.

The most important of these architects of the last two generations are by no means unknown in Europe. Names like Richardson, McKim, Mead, White, Cope, Stewardson, Day, Clipston, Shurges, Hastings, Carrière, and Cass Gilbert have a familiar ring. The buildings these men erected — one need only think of the libraries of Boston and Washington, the houses of delegates in Pittsburgh and Providence, the Metropolitan Club of New York, the universities in Philadelphia, Cambridge, and San Francisco — are embossed with the golden letters of the history of architecture.

To us, who regard the American architectural style with old-world eyes, four elements stand out. First is the imported English tradition, whether in the old colonial style or in modern form; then the French Beaux Arts style, for which Washington and Fifth Avenue in New York are representative examples. Added to these is a third element that emerged from purely practical consideration and found its expression in the skyscraper. Finally, however, there is a new spirit that emanates from America's modern works, a spirit that has found concrete forms on the Pacific Coast and in the Midwest.

Above all, this new spirit permeates the work of Frank Lloyd Wright. The charm and special attraction this new direction holds for us is probably the absence in these works of any reflection of the European forms to which we have long been accustomed. This turning away from tradition plus the particular manner of arrangement presuppose a unique style, a style that derives from the artist's pleasure in new material forms and in the liberal use of machine technology. The structures on the Pacific Coast, naturally, exhibit traits that deviate markedly from characteristics of the Chicago School, reflecting different conditions. I liked some of the houses I visited on the banks of the Aroyo River even better than those by Lloyd Wright; but the works of all the followers of the new direction share the above-mentioned characteristics, and Lloyd Wright's works show them in a more conspicuous and more sharply delineated form than those of any of his contemporaries. This is hardly surprising since the work he has done in the Midwest is the very epitome of innovative, original architectural design.

He received his training in the studio of Louis Sullivan, who, for his part, was the first to endow Chicago industrial buildings with a functional imprint. Lloyd Wright, however, applied the new direction to the construction of private buildings, thereby creating a new type of structure, completely independent of any foreign model, and enriching the city of the prairie with a new treasure, a new architectural style.

If one is to gain a true appreciation of this architect's achievements, one must take into consideration the difficulties he had to confront. He had no tradition to fall back on, he was not surrounded by forms out of which the new style could organically emerge; the milieu was purely entrepreneurial. Yet he withstood the virulent hostility of dangerous dilettantes and worked out his own style and principles at a time when the tidal wave of the English Arts and Crafts movement, the German Secession, and the European Arts Nouveaux had not yet reached America.

In the design of the Winslow house, dating from the year 1893, and several other houses of the early period, the emerging elements of his style can already be discerned. The most prominent characteristics of his style may be described this way: above all, elegance in the total conception — some of his designs have the simple clarity of medieval Gothic structures or the drafts of Bramante; then beautiful-

ly proportioned measures as can be seen in the Oak Park houses with long, firm horizontal lines; furthermore, a delicately developed sense for the effect of mass and colors as exemplified in the Unity Temple and the county house. Here his fertile imagination combines with a sense for practical details and he displays a firm determination, which sometimes reaches heroic proportions, to impress machine technology into the service of his goals — through forms and methods that are adaptable to the machine, but without disregarding traditional forms.

In 1908 Lloyd Wright formulated his principles in a very accessible, topically interesting monograph for the *Architectural Record* of New York. A few quotes from this article, entitled "In the Cause of Architecture," will explain his work very well:

> I make the same demands of an architectural work as I do of my fellow man, namely, that it be honest and true to itself. This main characteristic I wish to see combined with as much charm and grace as can be imagined.
>
> But most essential is inner integrity. The machine is the tool which uniquely characterizes our cultural epoch and creating a work that is fitting for this machine is an important task. Adapting a work to the potential of the machine is the content of the modern, industrial ideal which we must construct if architecture is not to lose its leading position within the realm of art.

Wright confronts us here with the very problem of our culture, whose solution will decide the future development of art in general. It is remarkable that here, completely independent of the old sites of culture in England, France, or Germany, a voice is sounded from Chicago that offers a solution to the artistic problem of our age. He says, furthermore:

> The staggering barriers are the artist's best friends. The machine can no longer be removed from the world; it is here to stay and is the pioneer of democracy, which is the ultimate goal of our hopes and desires. The architect of our time should know no more important task than the deployment of this modern tool as much as possible. But what does he do instead? He misuses this tool for the

creation of forms that arose in different times, under a distant sky, forms that today have a strangling effect because one cannot escape from them wherever one goes, and all this takes place with the help of the machine whose main task it is precisely to destroy these forms.

Wright expresses here a great idea, which, I believe, will prove fruitful in the future. He has turned this idea into action, and at the same time, he has advanced new specifications to which a modern building must conform.

But greatness is gained through sacrifices and these sacrifices often consist of a certain barrenness of detail, which in turn is the result of imposed limitations, recognizable in the disregard for all those intimate, personal imponderables that give a building its graceful form. All these sacrifices are made in deference to the cult of inner truthfulness, and it cannot be attributed as much to a mistake on the part of the architect as to the conditions under which he must labor. The dominance of the machine in modern life has not yet been fully established, and it often exceeds the strength of the individual (be he a giant) to exhaust the machine in all its facets. But it is a necessity of the totality, a social exigency, which is most clearly audible in American art.

Only in California does this spirit of the age assert itself more reticently. There the pulsebeat of life is quieter; the calming breath emanating from the Far East does not fail to exercise its influence on the inhabitants. Artists and architects are more at leisure to follow their train of thought. But for America in general, there is a barrier, and surmounting it within the framework of machine technology is an issue of life and death for American art. For in the United States, mechanical energy has destroyed the traditions of craftsmanship on which art is based. And to this day, despite superior organizational talent and almost limitless resources, American architects have not been able to resurrect what was lost. By the same token, they have not succeeded in finding a suitable substitute to fill the void that was left. Of all Americans, it was Lloyd Wright who first recognized most clearly and consciously the need that has thus crystallized. He must, therefore, be credited with having made a major contribution, and the way he presents

DANA HOUSE, SPRINGFIELD, ILL.: TERRACOTTA FIGURE FOR THE ENTRANCE; FRANK LLOYD WRIGHT, ARCHITECT; RICHARD BOCK, SCULPTOR.

himself in Chicago reveals him as the prototype of the modern American, a true product of his surroundings.

We perceive in him the very strength and weakness — the poetic charm, the capriciousness and immaturity, or even infertility, side by side with robust health and a wealth of natural resources — that characterize his country. Yes, one may well say his character exhibits the indigenous personality traits of the country itself. By personality I understand Murray's definition of individualism, which states: Individualism is acting and feeling, a way of living through which the individual strives for the achievement of his own goals and ideas.

Why individualism took its most extreme form in Chicago, of all places, I am unable to say; but every street, every avenue of this brutal, inconsiderate yet open-hearted and generous city sings its praises. It sounds the song of destiny of the New Englander who went West and there, freed from all constraints, built his home in a commercial world, or the song of the Puritan who has been cut off from the soil in which his gods and customs had grown and who now proudly gives life to new gods and new customs. His striving is, as William Blake the seer said, "to create a system that frees the individual from systems." More than any of the works of his contemporaries, it is in Frank Lloyd Wright's work that this striving is most clearly revealed.

This style, one must admit without losing sight of the influence Louis Sullivan exercised on its development, is first and foremost Lloyd Wright's work. Fate endowed this man with a will to create, and whenever he is engaged in his endeavor, it seems to scorn him and collect in the end a few fragments of his works — all that is truly great and seemingly made to last — for use in the great task that still lies ahead of mankind. Thus emerges a new style in all artistic endeavors, but above all in architecture.

A dominant figure will be easily forgiven for a slip of the reins at times so that his individualism breaks through the barriers, but a minor figure will never receive the same consideration. What is regarded as character in one appears as caprice and vain mannerism in the other. And may we European architects not be taken to task if we, in appreciating, criticizing, and admiring, sometimes deplore the lack of a

DANA HOUSE, SPRINGFIELD, ILL.: ENTRANCE.

certain maturity in these expressions of individualism? But no matter what our position may be, we must take this into account as a given condition in which a people unfolds its essence. As an architect, I would like to say that individualism in Lloyd Wright's work appears strong and healthy to the core, but I don't always like it. I am sometimes overcome by the same vexing feeling that forces itself on me when reading Walt Whitman. When the poet, after making my heart open up with a particular expression, suddenly stumbles over a banality that he has not mastered (as when he calls out at the end of his magnificent song "Come I will make the continent indissoluble": "for you Democracy — Ma Femme!"), he overlooks the fact that we too are made of flesh and blood and have a sense of humor, even if unintended, and that with this trivial exclamation he tosses us from the heights of poetry to the depths of poorly executed details.

I don't mean to insinuate with this analogy that Lloyd Wright's works exhibit such deviousness. Like all analogies, this one too is limping, of course, and my statement is only meant to serve as an opening into a feeling I am unable to fend off whenever my eyes encounter a triviality. In this context, I would like to say that Lloyd Wright's architectural work justifies the comparison with Whitman's literary work insofar as greatness and coherence are concerned and that it possesses sufficient inner strength and firmness to hold up under criticism that points up its weaknesses and errors.

It would be going beyond the purview of this study if I were to draw parallels between Wright's work and that of modern English or German architects, but a certain inner kinship cannot be denied, and several well-known names come to mind: in Germany there are Olbrich, Hoffmann, Moser, Bruno Paul, Möhring; in England, the so-called Arts and Crafts men like Lethaby, Voysey, Lutyens, Ricardo, Wilson, Holden, Blow, Townsend, Baillie, Scott.

Our kinship does not lie so much in the means of expression. In fact, we differ considerably in overall approach, in the finishing touches to our work; our sense of rhythm is a different one, as are our problems from those faced by Lloyd Wright. But we are in agreement on basic principles. Together we shield the eternal fire of truth, together we honor the idea that a building must be understandable in and of itself — that iron exists to serve man, provided he has learned to use it and defies any attempt to mask or obscure its presence.

The old-world forms, the Beaux Arts tradition, the old colonial style, as well as a "purely" Greek style, all have their place in the world, but this place need not be the prairie. They may come into their own in Cincinnati or Virginia, on the Boulevard Montparnasse or in Buckinghamshire, but they are not suitable to vast, endless spaces of the New World. This land, crisscrossed by an extensive network of railroad tracks in the Midwest, with its new cities founded by miners, by cattle breeders, by men who conserve meat and export grain, by men full of inventive ideas — this land poses special, new challenges.

Whatever we may think of those men who made this land what it is today, they did create something new, and the time has come for new forms of expression that are relevant to their lives and the lives they seek to build. Absent from their lives is any kind of pettiness, and this may be why Lloyd Wright's works contain a coherence and generosity, as revealed in his draft designs. I felt this myself when entering his buildings, such as the Coonley house in Chicago and the Larkin building in Buffalo. The architect's mission is to give expression to life and by doing so to ennoble it. Even though Lloyd Wright lives for this ideal, it is, nevertheless, necessary to remember that he cannot lay claim to recognition only for himself. An examination of his buildings and drawings teaches us how much he owes to those who commissioned his work — his clients. They too were filled by a sense of capaciousness and sought to give it expression. This is especially true of the Larkin building in Buffalo. It is impossible to rid oneself of the feeling that the magnificence of the business organization provided the artist with the stimulus for his magnificent work.

With hungry eyes we Europeans regard our more fortunate colleagues of the New World, their wonderful spatial relationships and vast stretches of uninhabited territory, their cities that still await the artist's hand and the generosity of the sponsors. But we envy them all this less than the breath of new life, which, unhampered by traditions and customs, is able to pulse so much more freely than here where we immediately feel the fetters as soon as we attempt to express our ideas in wood and stone,

COONLEY HOUSE, RIVERSIDE, ILL.

iron, and concrete. The reason for this is easy to see. How different is the life of an American sponsor from that of a European magnate, how much freer, less constricted, inspired by greater ideas. But it must also be said how much more vulgar, perhaps even rougher, is this life. Your American desires a spacious room, flights of rooms kept at the same temperature; he desires concentration — haste is his life's element; he lacks a sense for musing but appreciates the costly work of a pipe fitter, and with truly childlike eagerness he buys up all the bric-a-brac of Europe that he can gather.

A very different mentality prevails among the affluent in England and Germany. Their limitations are more clearly drawn. The wealthy bourgeois German does not merely feel the emperor's protective hand. He may not even love his emperor, but the emperor wears a uniform and represents another dimension. He is a looming, luminous figure beyond reality, something unattainable, in glittering colors and gold. In England, it is the House of Lords with all its pitfalls that dominates the milieu of the landed gentry, whose influence rests heavily on the construction and decoration of a planned house. An English gentleman would believe himself to be indulging in lowly and costly passions if he were to pay the bill of an American pipe-fitter, which in the case of a large building could run into several thousands. He would fear that he might be undermining the discipline of the servants and that he might hurt the most sacred feelings of his horses.

The same difference can be found with regard to public buildings. England is the most democratic of the three countries, whereby I understand the word in the sense of Abraham Lincoln. Germany exhibits the strictest discipline, and in America the power of money, or the man who owns it, rules unchallenged. Consequently, when it comes to the construction of English public buildings, the committee, on which small shopkeepers serve, has the decisive say. Their world of ideas is ruled by sixpence, and thus we often arrive at conclusions that evoke in us a certain melancholy. In America, the dominant "boss system" often, though not always, places the most capable man on the top, while in Germany, by contrast, life is ruled by a tightly knit tradition, which subsequently finds its expression in the country's architecture as well.

From a psychological standpoint, it seems logical that these forces of life, briefly sketched here, should leave their imprint on the three countries, and we must examine our common basis for familiar traits. We artists are easily inclined to regard ourselves as discoverers of forms that we present to the world as something new. But that is not so. Rather it is as tools of the *Zeitgeist*, of the world soul, that we perform our work.

In each one of our works, one can detect the same lines of hasty, nervous movement, the same great massive formations, the same sense of relationships within established confines, the flight from tradition, from monotony, from constant mechanical repetition, the search for personal expression in order to escape the routine.

COONLEY HOUSE, RIVERSIDE, ILL.

In our time, all this has a psychological basis. We must only call to mind the concentration of industry, the rapid conquest of space, the telephone, electricity, wire transmitters, cheap mechanical energy. The resulting changes in working conditions compel the old, obsolete system of production to declare its bankruptcy. In addition, there are the telegraph, photography, the advances of the press, especially of illustrated magazines, and all those manifestations of modern times that, even if unconsciously, leave their effect on us. They speak through us as if we were puppets on the stage of the world theater, they guide us in mysterious ways, and, apparently most incomprehensible to the individual, they cause us to communicate in a common, universally understood tongue.

Let me repeat: a style develops organically, and the style of the twentieth century would, therefore, be lacking in essence and reality were it not to reflect the currents that form the background against which modern life unfolds.

So far, Lloyd Wright has not had the opportunity to try his hand at public buildings, but the structures that bear his signature bear witness to his personality. No one who has seen the Unity Temple of Oak Park, who has taken pleasure in its monumental character — the revival of the temple form of antiquity, which seems quite suitable for a modern cult — can escape the impression that here a new, specifically American spirit has been at work. In hundreds of years to come, at a time when the

entire suburb that surrounds the iron-concrete monolith has long vanished, it will persist and endure.

I am purposely refraining from elaborating on details of the interior design of Lloyd Wright's structures, for this is not the focus of his work. This is not what typifies him. It is the machine he seeks to master, and herein are the limitations of his power.

Frequently, traces of Japanese influence can be detected. His endeavor to adapt Japanese forms to American conditions are clearly discernible even though the artist is unwilling to admit this source. No doubt the East Asian influence is an unconscious one, but I see it in most of his architectural drawings and his manner of showcasing the picturesque element of his works. To me these structures have great charm and some of the illustrations in this volume convey his achievements in interior design through the use of materials such as glass and fabrics. Even carpentry and furniture are among his creations. All these details deserve our admiration, especially the logical way in which they are adapted to the total structure — even if, for our European taste, they do not constitute as convincing a testimony of his genius as the buildings themselves. However, here too his principles are of a most refined nature. This is most clearly expressed in his own words:

> In order to form a structure, its environment, and interior appointment into a harmonious whole, the accessories

9

must be subordinated to the overall purpose; may this purpose be artistic or practical, the structure in its totality must absorb it. It is the job of the architect to make it conform to the true nature of the structure. This is the primary task of the modern architect. He must be able to mold the structure into a self-contained, harmonious work of art which reflects the work and sentiments of its inhabitants and thus becomes an artist's act of revelation that permits his genius to shine through the material and design.

Successive generations had appointed Romanesque churches of the Old World with mosaics, tracery, and all the luxury of an emergent culture and its growing taste for more leisure. It may be that in centuries to come the same will happen to American architecture, which today still appears to us as an experiment.

I have in mind particularly certain works by Lloyd Wright that I would like to touch with a magic wand. Their inner structure should remain, but I would adorn them in a gentler, more vivid manner. How this would be done, I don't know. The time for this has not yet come and I would not want to see Wright himself trying his hand at this, for I don't believe he could succeed. For the kind of adornment I am envisioning presupposes the existence of a well-developed Arts and Crafts movement, reflecting the indigenous culture of America. It would breathe some of the calm, the poetic charm, and the mature experience of our English churches and castles, which were created by the loving hands of generations of artists.

However this may be, the illustrations in these pages show buildings.

[William] Morris once said to me, speaking on behalf of a certain elegant ornament, "We shall dispense with it unless the building to which it will be affixed is an elegant one itself."

Frank Lloyd Wright's architectural works live up to this idea.

Translated from the German by
BRIGITTE M. GOLDSTEIN

LARKIN BUILDING: CASING; FRANK LLOYD WRIGHT, ARCHITECT;
RICHARD BOCK, SCULPTOR.

UNITY TEMPLE, OAK PARK, ILL.

UNITY TEMPLE AND UNITY HOUSE, OAK PARK, ILL.

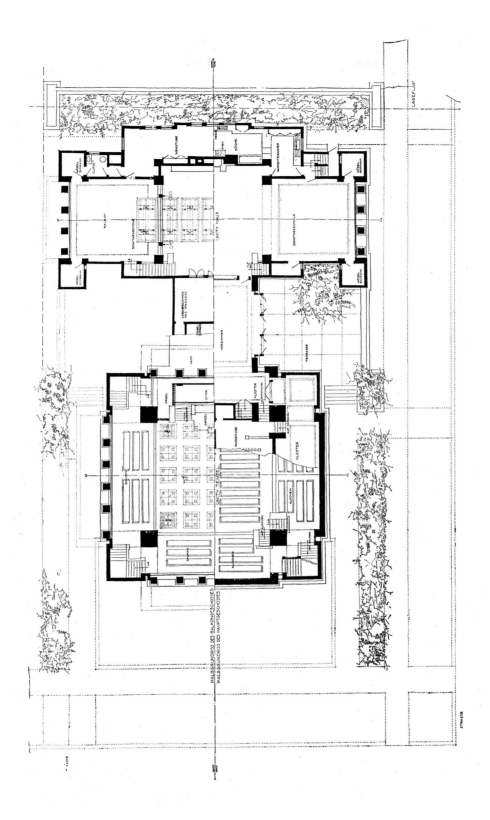

UNITY TEMPLE AND UNITY HOUSE, OAK PARK, ILL.: GROUND PLAN.

13

UNITY TEMPLE AND UNITY HOUSE, OAK PARK, ILL.

14

UNITY TEMPLE, OAK PARK, ILL.: WEST FACADE (TOP AND BOTTOM).

15

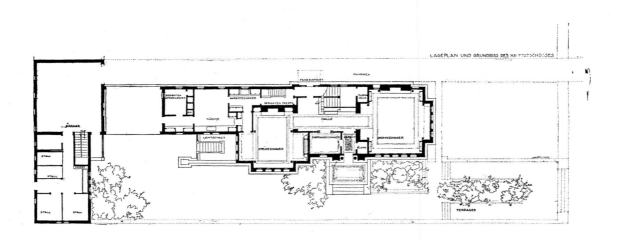

UNITY TEMPLE, OAK PARK, ILL.: INTERIOR (TOP).
ISIDOR HELLER TOWN HOUSE, WOODLAWN AVENUE, CHICAGO, ILL., 1896: GROUND PLAN (BOTTOM).

16

ISIDOR HELLER TOWN HOUSE, CHICAGO, ILL.

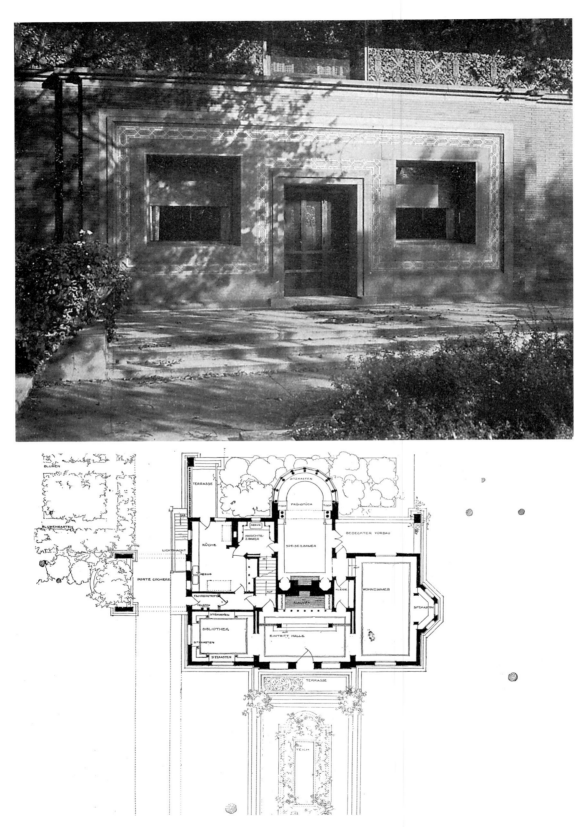

W. H. WINSLOW HOUSE, RIVER FOREST, ILL., 1893: ENTRANCE (TOP) AND GROUND PLAN (BOTTOM).

W. H. WINSLOW HOUSE, RIVER FOREST, ILL.

HUSSER MANSION, BUENA PARK, CHICAGO, ILL., 1898.

HUSSER MANSION, CHICAGO, ILL.: WEST FACADE (TOP) AND SOUTH FACADE (BOTTOM).

21

WILLIAMS MANSION, RIVER FOREST, ILL., 1894.

B. HARLEY BRADLEY HOUSE, KANKAKEE, ILL., 1900.

B. HARLEY BRADLEY HOUSE, KANKAKEE, ILL.: ENTRANCEWAY (TOP) AND DINING ROOM (BOTTOM).

B. HARLEY BRADLEY HOUSE, KANKAKEE, ILL.: LIVING ROOM.

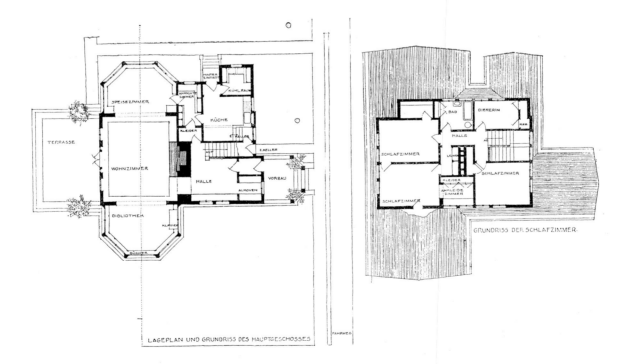

WARREN HICKOX HOUSE, KANKAKEE, ILL., 1900: SOUTH FACADE (TOP)
AND GROUND PLAN (BOTTOM).

26

WARREN HICKOX HOUSE, KANKAKEE, ILL.: EAST FACADE.

27

THOMAS HOUSE, OAK PARK, ILL., 1902.

THOMAS HOUSE, OAK PARK, ILL.: DETAILS OF THE EAST FACADE (TOP AND BOTTOM).

29

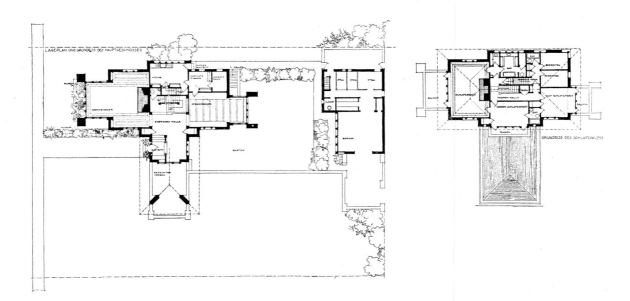

F. W. LITTLE COUNTRY HOUSE, PEORIA, ILL., 1900: ENTRANCE (TOP) AND GROUND PLAN (BOTTOM).

F. W. LITTLE COUNTRY HOUSE, PEORIA, ILL.

SUSAN L. DANA HOUSE, SPRINGFIELD, ILL., 1899.

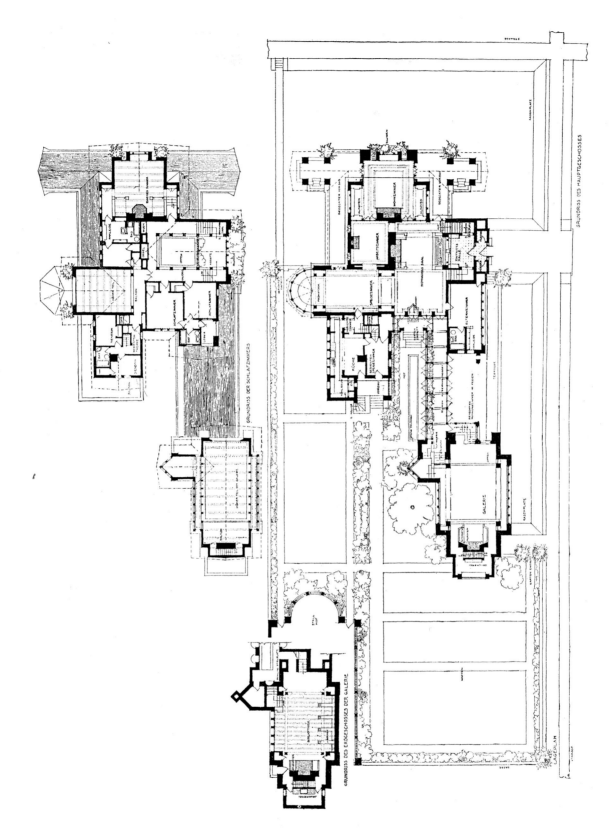

SUSAN L. DANA HOUSE, SPRINGFIELD, ILL.: GROUND PLANS OF THE MAIN AND UPPER FLOORS.

33

SUSAN L. DANA HOUSE, SPRINGFIELD, ILL.: SOUTH FACADE.

SUSAN L. DANA HOUSE, SPRINGFIELD, ILL.: DETAILS OF THE ENTRANCE FACADE (TOP AND BOTTOM).

SUSAN L. DANA HOUSE, SPRINGFIELD, ILL.: DINING ROOM.

SUSAN L. DANA HOUSE, SPRINGFIELD, ILL.: FOUNTAIN IN THE DINING ROOM.

SUSAN L. DANA HOUSE, SPRINGFIELD, ILL.: VIEWS OF THE DINING ROOM (TOP)
AND BREAKFAST NICHE (BOTTOM).

SUSAN L. DANA HOUSE, SPRINGFIELD, ILL.: EAST FACADE.

SUSAN L. DANA HOUSE, SPRINGFIELD, ILL.: EAST FACADE.

SUSAN L. DANA HOUSE, SPRINGFIELD, ILL.: DOUBLE DOOR (BOTTOM) AND GALLERY (TOP).

SUSAN L. DANA HOUSE, SPRINGFIELD, ILL.: EXTERIOR OF THE GALLERY.

SUSAN L. DANA HOUSE, SPRINGFIELD, ILL.: INTERIOR OF THE GALLERY.

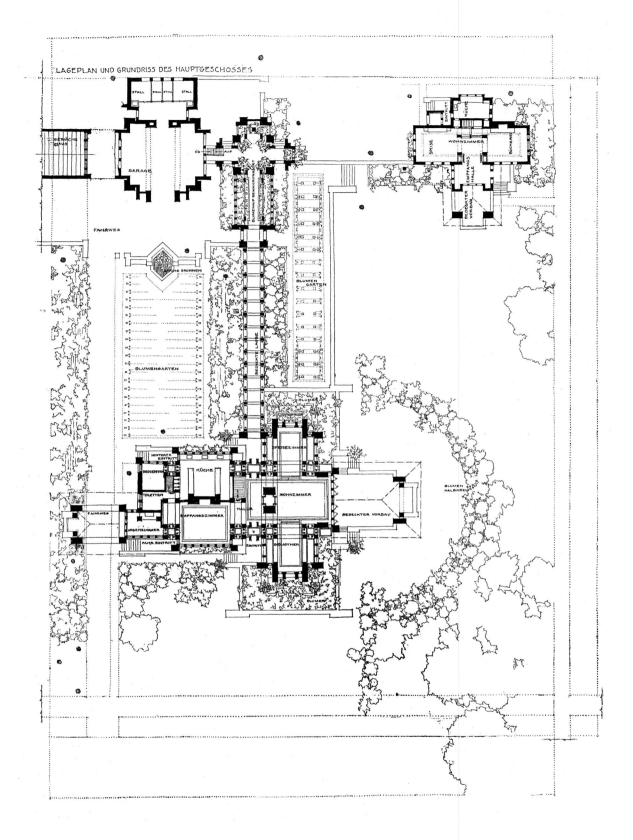

LAGEPLAN UND GRUNDRISS DES HAUPTGESCHOSSES

D. D. MARTIN HOUSE, BUFFALO, N.Y.: GROUND PLAN OF THE MAIN FLOOR.

44

D. D. MARTIN HOUSE, BUFFALO, N.Y.: BIRD'S-EYE VIEW.

D. D. MARTIN HOUSE, BUFFALO, N.Y.

D. D. MARTIN HOUSE, BUFFALO, N.Y.: HEATING UNIT WITH LIGHTING FIXTURES (BOTTOM)
AND CONSERVATORY (TOP).

47

D. D. MARTIN HOUSE, BUFFALO, N.Y.: PERGOLA (TOP) AND ENTRANCE HALL (BOTTOM).

D. D. MARTIN HOUSE, BUFFALO, N.Y.: CONSERVATORY (TOP) AND BIRDHOUSE (BOTTOM).

D. D. MARTIN HOUSE, BUFFALO, N.Y.: FIREPLACE IN THE LIVING ROOM.

D. D. MARTIN HOUSE, BUFFALO, N.Y.: DRAWING ROOM (TOP) AND DINING ROOM (BOTTOM).

D. D. MARTIN HOUSE, BUFFALO, N.Y.: WEST FACADE (TOP AND BOTTOM).

D. D. MARTIN HOUSE, BUFFALO, N.Y.: LIVING ROOM WITH HEATING UNIT AND LIGHTING FIXTURES.

53

D. D. MARTIN HOUSE, BUFFALO, N.Y.

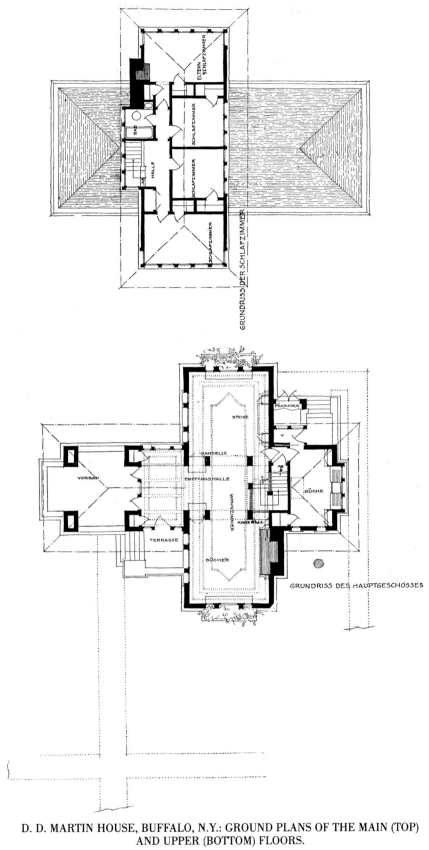

GRUNDRISS DER SCHLAFZIMMER

ELTERN SCHLAFZIMMER
SCHLAFZIMMER
SCHLAFZIMMER
BAD
HALLE
SCHLAFZIMMER

SPEISE
FAHRRÄDER
KANZELLE
EMPFANGSHALLE
KÜCHE
VORBAU
WOHNZIMMER
KANZELLE
TERRASSE
BÜCHER

GRUNDRISS DES HAUPTGESCHOSSES

D. D. MARTIN HOUSE, BUFFALO, N.Y.: GROUND PLANS OF THE MAIN (TOP)
AND UPPER (BOTTOM) FLOORS.

55

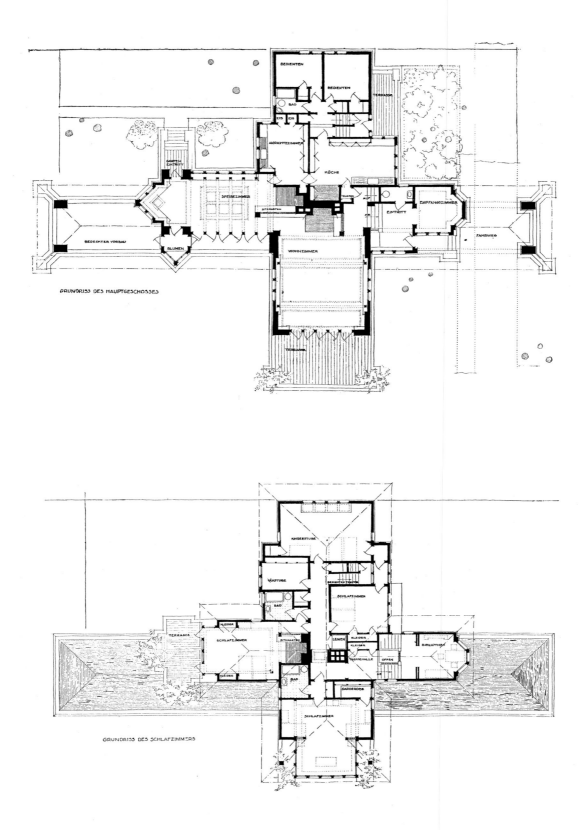

WARD W. WILLITS HOUSE, HIGHLAND PARK, ILL., 1903: GROUND PLANS OF THE UPPER (TOP)
AND MAIN (BOTTOM) FLOORS.

56

WARD W. WILLITS HOUSE, HIGHLAND PARK, ILL.

WARD W. WILLITS HOUSE, HIGHLAND PARK, ILL.: STREET FACADE.

WARD W. WILLITS HOUSE, HIGHLAND PARK, ILL.: ENTRANCE WING (TOP)
AND LIVING ROOM (BOTTOM).

59

OSCAR STEFFENS HOUSE, BIRCHWOOD, ILL., 1909.

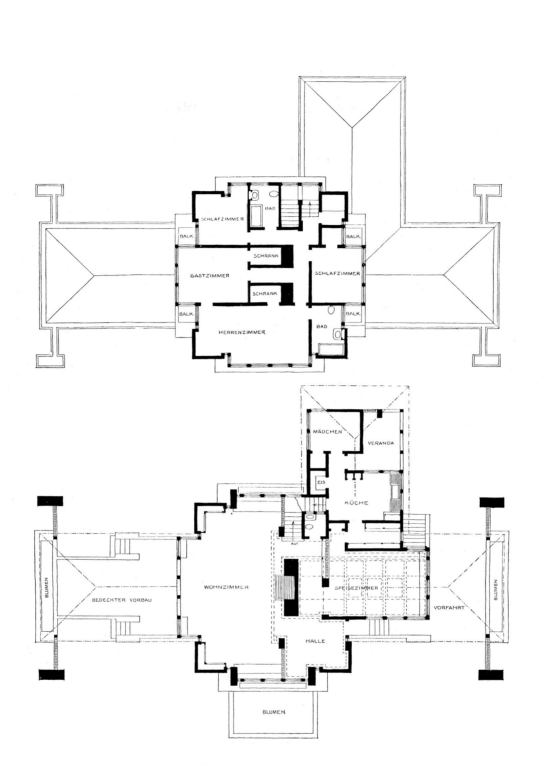

OSCAR STEFFENS HOUSE, BIRCHWOOD, ILL.: GROUND PLANS OF THE MAIN (TOP)
AND UPPER (BOTTOM) FLOORS.

61

HORNER HOUSE, BIRCHWOOD, ILL., 1908: EXTERIOR (TOP)
AND INTERIOR FACING THE ENTRANCE (BOTTOM).

62

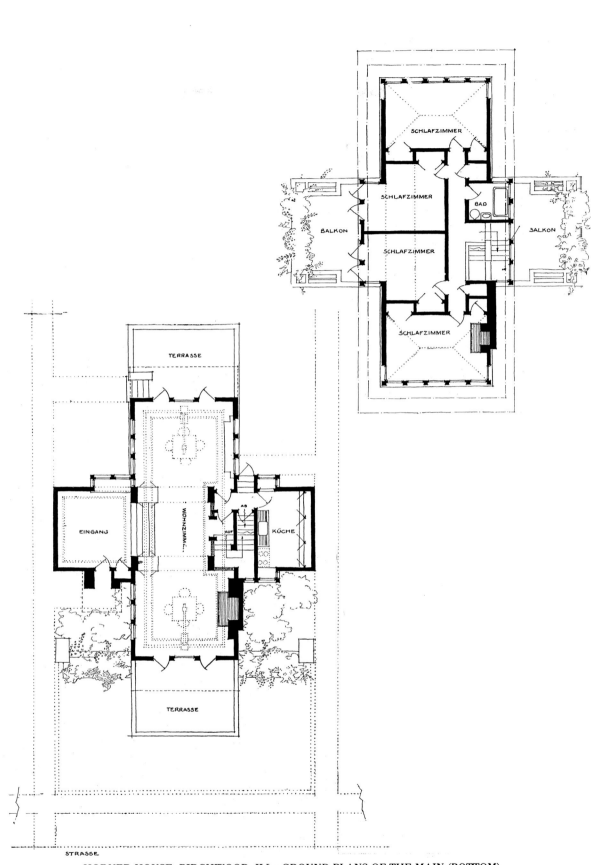

HORNER HOUSE, BIRCHWOOD, ILL.: GROUND PLANS OF THE MAIN (BOTTOM)
AND UPPER (TOP) FLOORS.

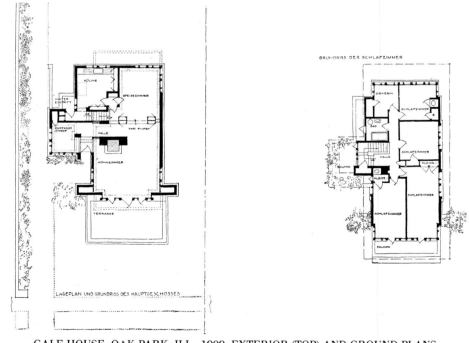

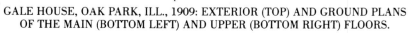

GALE HOUSE, OAK PARK, ILL., 1909: EXTERIOR (TOP) AND GROUND PLANS
OF THE MAIN (BOTTOM LEFT) AND UPPER (BOTTOM RIGHT) FLOORS.

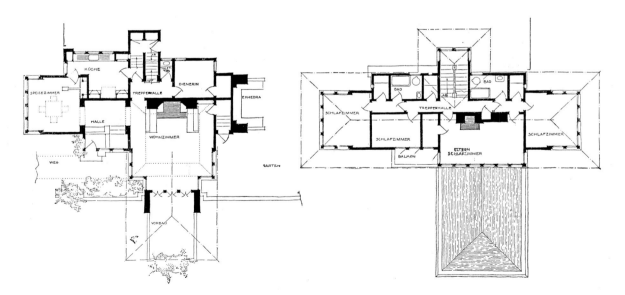

GEORGE MILLARD HOUSE, HIGHLAND PARK, ILL., 1906: EXTERIOR (TOP)
AND GROUND PLANS OF THE MAIN (BOTTOM LEFT) AND UPPER (BOTTOM RIGHT) FLOORS.

ISABEL ROBERTS COUNTRY HOUSE, RIVER FOREST, ILL., 1908.

ISABEL ROBERTS COUNTRY HOUSE, RIVER FOREST, ILL.: SOUTH FACADE (TOP)
AND LIVING ROOM (BOTTOM).

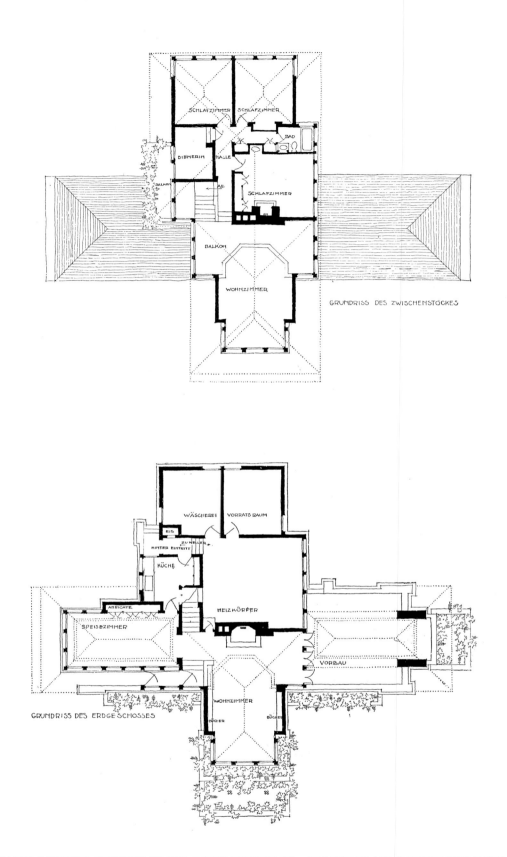

ISABEL ROBERTS COUNTRY HOUSE, RIVER FOREST, ILL.: GROUND PLANS OF THE MAIN (BOTTOM)
AND UPPER (TOP) FLOORS.

68

MARTIN MANSION, OAK PARK, ILL., 1904: GARDEN VIEWS (TOP AND BOTTOM).

69

TOMEK MANSION, RIVERSIDE, ILL., 1907: STREET FACADE.

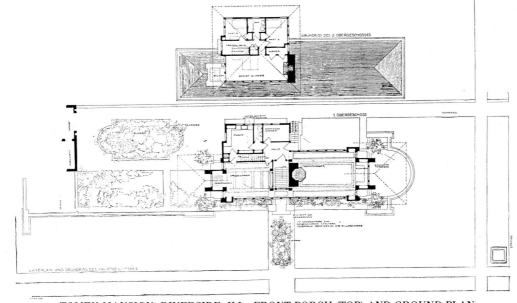

TOMEK MANSION, RIVERSIDE, ILL.: FRONT PORCH (TOP) AND GROUND PLAN.

EMMA MARTIN HOUSE, OAK PARK, ILL., 1901.

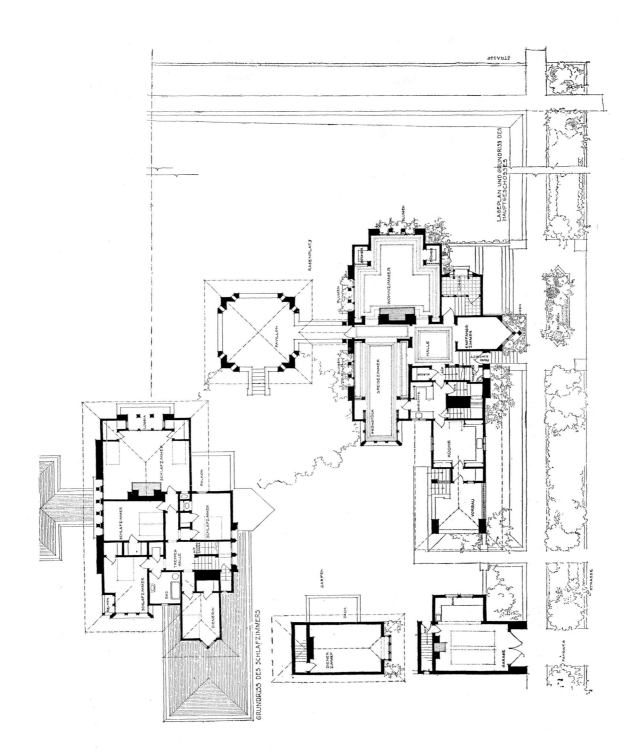

EMMA MARTIN HOUSE, OAK PARK, ILL.: GROUND PLANS OF THE MAIN AND UPPER FLOORS.

EMMA MARTIN HOUSE, OAK PARK, ILL.: PAVILION (TOP) AND GARDEN (BOTTOM) FACADES.

EMMA MARTIN HOUSE, OAK PARK, ILL.: STREET FACADE.

BEACHY MANSION, OAK PARK, ILL.: GARDEN FACADE.

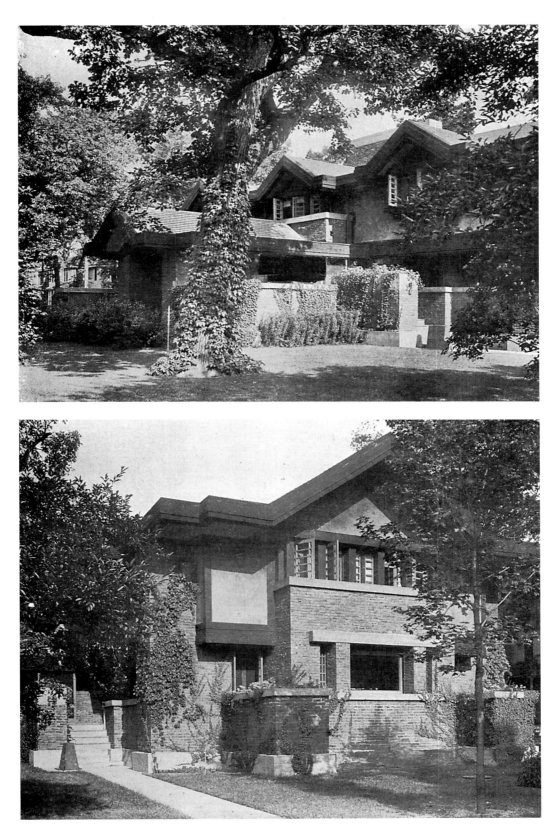

BEACHY MANSION, OAK PARK, ILL.: GARDEN (TOP) AND STREET (BOTTOM) FACADES.

W. R. HEATH TOWN HOUSE, BUFFALO, N.Y., 1903.

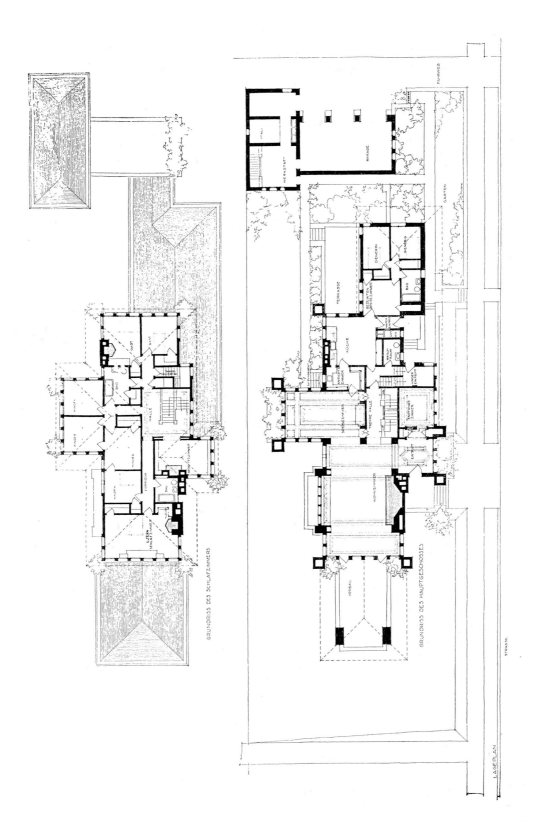

W. R. HEATH TOWN HOUSE, BUFFALO, N.Y.: GROUND PLANS OF THE MAIN (LEFT)
AND UPPER (RIGHT) FLOORS.

W. R. HEATH TOWN HOUSE, BUFFALO, N.Y.: ENTRANCE FACADE (TOP AND BOTTOM).

W. R. HEATH TOWN HOUSE, BUFFALO, N.Y.: LIVING ROOM.

W. R. HEATH TOWN HOUSE, BUFFALO, N.Y.: FIREPLACE (TOP).
SUSAN L. DANA HOUSE, SPRINGFIELD, ILL.: FIRE SCREEN (BOTTOM).

ROBERT EVANS HOUSE, LONGWOOD, ILL., 1909: FIREPLACE IN THE LIVING ROOM (TOP).
B. HARLEY BRADLEY HOUSE, KANKAKEE, ILL.: FIREPLACE IN THE LIVING ROOM (BOTTOM).

ROBERT EVANS HOUSE, LONGWOOD, ILL.

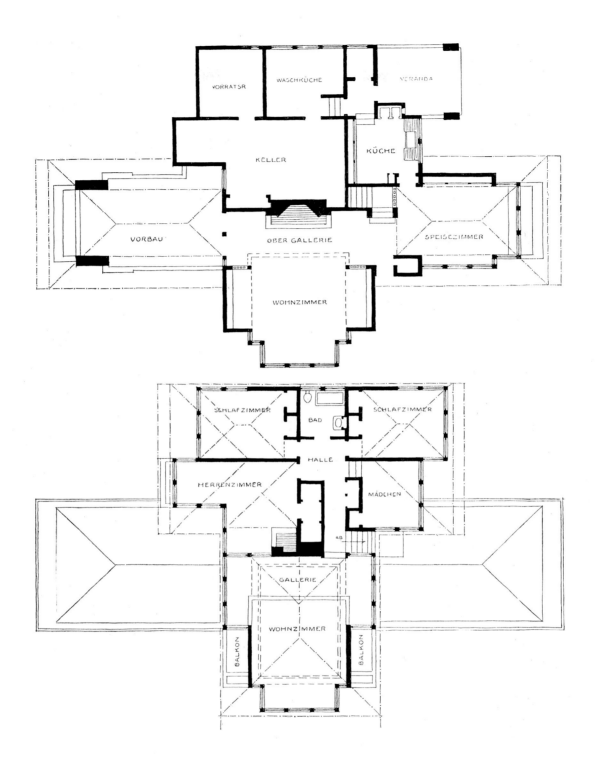

ROBERT EVANS HOUSE, LONGWOOD, ILL.: GROUND PLANS OF THE MAIN (BOTTOM)
AND UPPER (TOP) FLOORS.

85

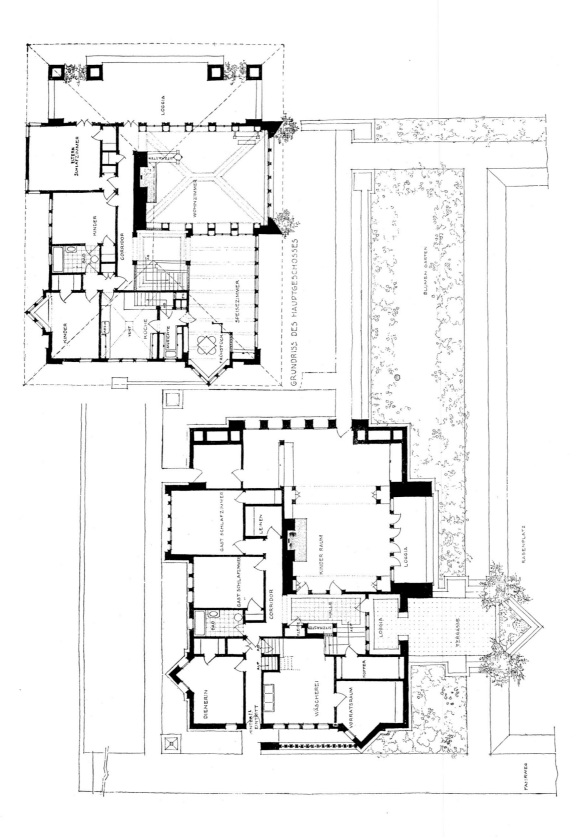

ARTHUR HEURTLEY HOUSE, OAK PARK, ILL., 1901: GROUND PLANS OF THE MAIN (RIGHT)
AND UPPER (LEFT) FLOORS.

86

ARTHUR HEURTLEY HOUSE, OAK PARK, ILL.: STREET FACADE (TOP) AND UPPER HALL (BOTTOM).

ARTHUR HEURTLEY HOUSE, OAK PARK, ILL.: NORTH (TOP) AND SOUTH (BOTTOM) FACADES.

ARTHUR HEURTLEY HOUSE, OAK PARK, ILL.: STREET FACADE.

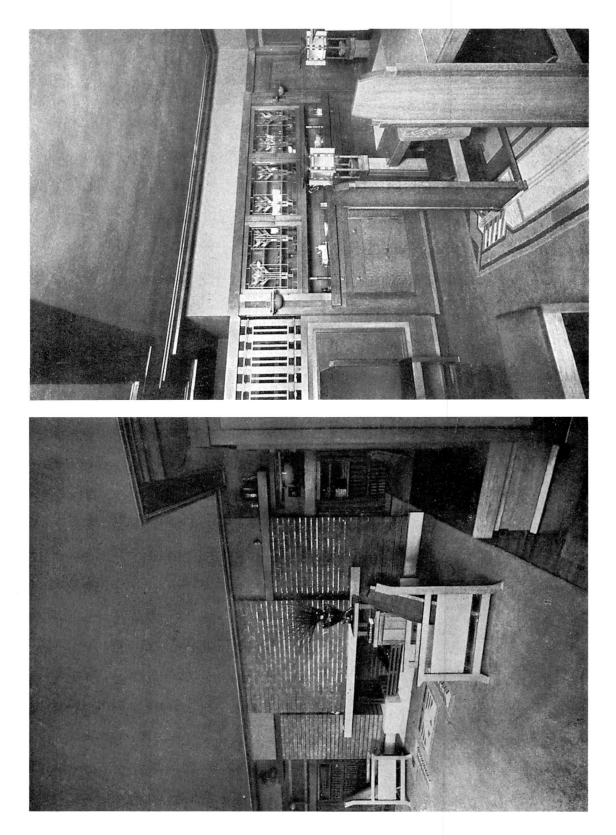

MEYER MAY HOUSE, GRAND RAPIDS, MICH., 1909: FIREPLACE IN THE LIVING ROOM (BOTTOM) AND DINING ROOM (TOP).

MEYER MAY HOUSE, GRAND RAPIDS, MICH.

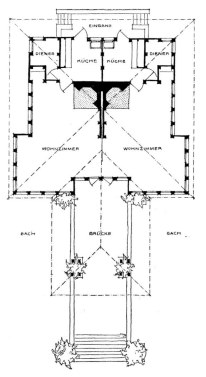

GEORGE E. GERTS TWIN SUMMER HOUSE, WHITEHALL, MICH.: EXTERIOR (TOP)
AND GROUND PLAN (BOTTOM).

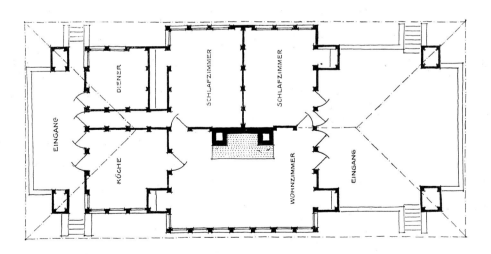

WALTER GERTS SUMMER HOUSE, WHITEHALL, MICH., 1902: EXTERIOR (TOP)
AND GROUND PLAN (BOTTOM).

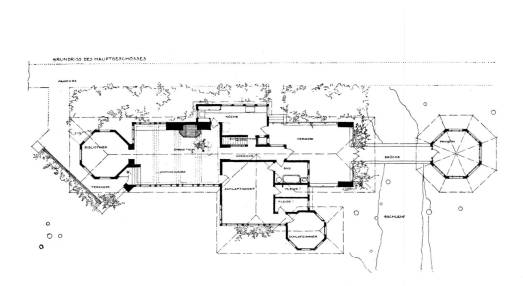

W. A. GLASNER COUNTRY HOUSE, GLENCOE, ILL.: EXTERIOR (TOP) AND GROUND PLAN (BOTTOM).

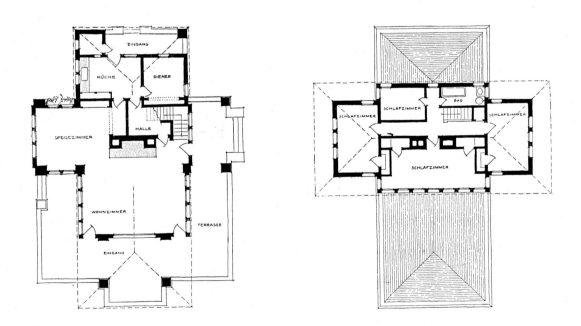

CHARLES ROSS SUMMER HOUSE, LAKE DELAVAN, WISC.: EXTERIOR (TOP)
AND GROUND PLAN (BOTTOM).

FRANK J. BAKER MANSION, WITMETH, ILL., 1909: STREET FACADE.

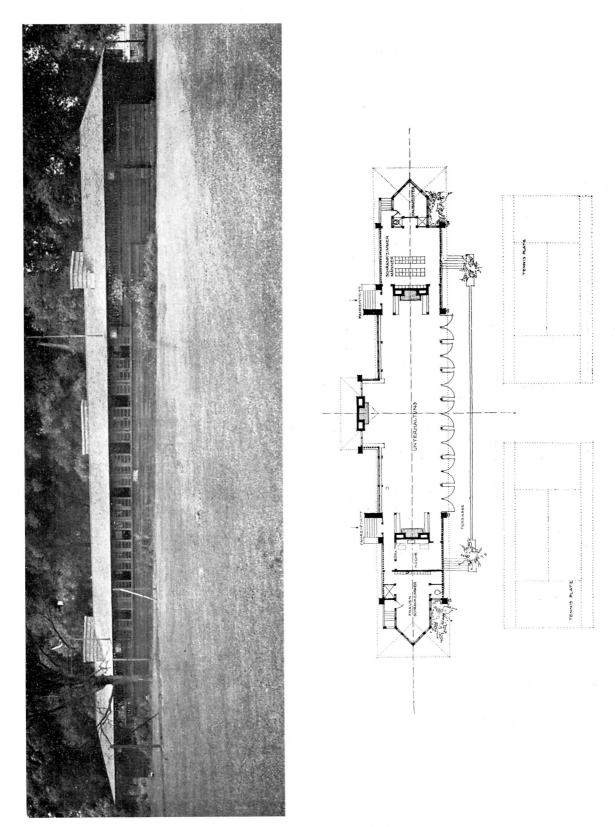

RIVER FOREST TENNIS CLUB, RIVER FOREST, ILL., 1906: EXTERIOR (LEFT)
AND GROUND PLAN (RIGHT).

FRANK LLOYD WRIGHT STUDIO, OAK PARK, ILL.: PORTRAIT FIGURE BY RICHARD BOCK, SCULPTOR.

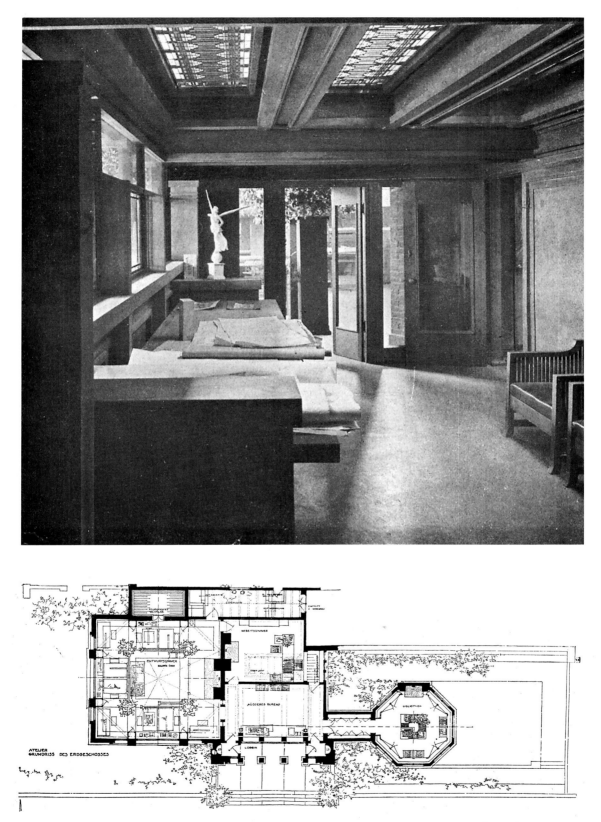

FRANK LLOYD WRIGHT STUDIO, OAK PARK, ILL.: OUTER OFFICE (TOP) AND GROUND PLAN (BOTTOM).

BROWNE'S BOOKSTORE, FINE ARTS BUILDING, CHICAGO, ILL., 1907.

SPECIAL EXHIBIT OF DRAWINGS AND MODELS AT THE CHICAGO ART INSTITUTE, CHICAGO, ILL., 1907.

SPECIAL EXHIBIT OF DRAWINGS AND MODELS AT THE CHICAGO ART INSTITUTE, CHICAGO, ILL.

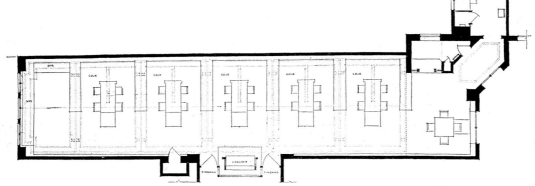

SPECIAL EXHIBIT OF DRAWINGS AND MODELS AT THE CHICAGO ART INSTITUTE, CHICAGO, ILL. (TOP).
BROWNE'S BOOKSTORE, CHICAGO, ILL.: GROUND PLAN (BOTTOM).

BROWNE'S BOOKSTORE, CHICAGO, ILL.: INTERIOR (TOP).
FRANK LLOYD WRIGHT STUDIO, CHICAGO, ILL.: DETAIL OF THE ENTRANCE (BOTTOM).

BROWNE'S BOOKSTORE, CHICAGO, ILL.: CASHIER'S COUNTER (TOP).
FRANK LLOYD WRIGHT STUDIO, CHICAGO, ILL.: ENTRANCE (BOTTOM).

BROWNE'S BOOKSTORE, CHICAGO, ILL.: INTERIOR (TOP).
FRANK LLOYD WRIGHT STUDIO, CHICAGO, ILL.: LIBRARY (BOTTOM).

BROWNE'S BOOKSTORE, CHICAGO, ILL.: DISPLAY WINDOW AND ENTRANCE (TOP)
AND READING ROOM (BOTTOM).

FRANK LLOYD WRIGHT STUDIO, CHICAGO, ILL.: WORKROOM.

THURBER ART GALLERY FOR PAINTINGS AND ETCHINGS (TOP AND BOTTOM).

D. D. MARTIN HOUSE, BUFFALO, N.Y.: FIREPLACE WALL IN GOLD-GLASS MOSAIC.

EXHIBITION AT MADISON SQUARE GARDEN, NEW YORK CITY, 1910: DESIGN IN CEMENT AND TILES.

FRED C. ROBIE TOWN HOUSE, WOODLAWN AVENUE, CHICAGO, ILL., 1906: SOUTH FACADE.

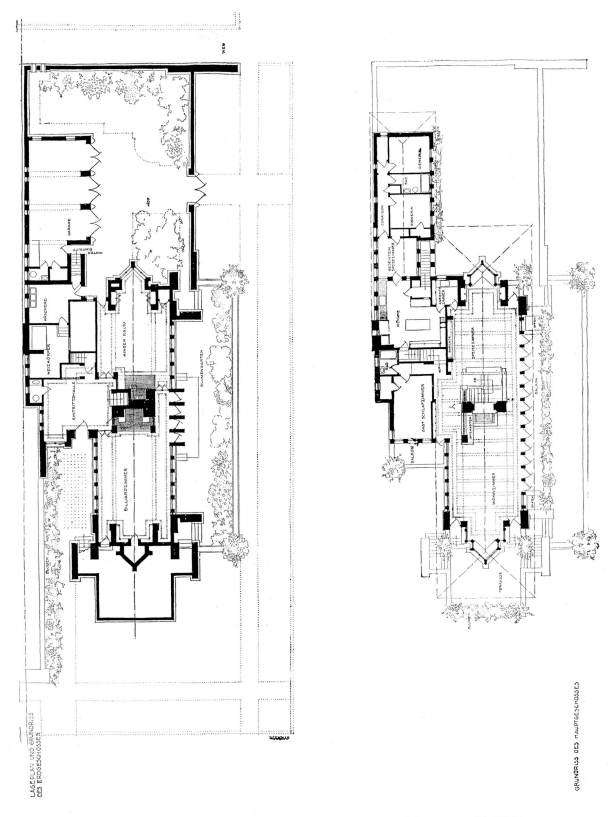

FRED C. ROBIE TOWN HOUSE, CHICAGO, ILL.: GROUND PLANS OF THE MAIN (LEFT)
AND UPPER (RIGHT) FLOORS.

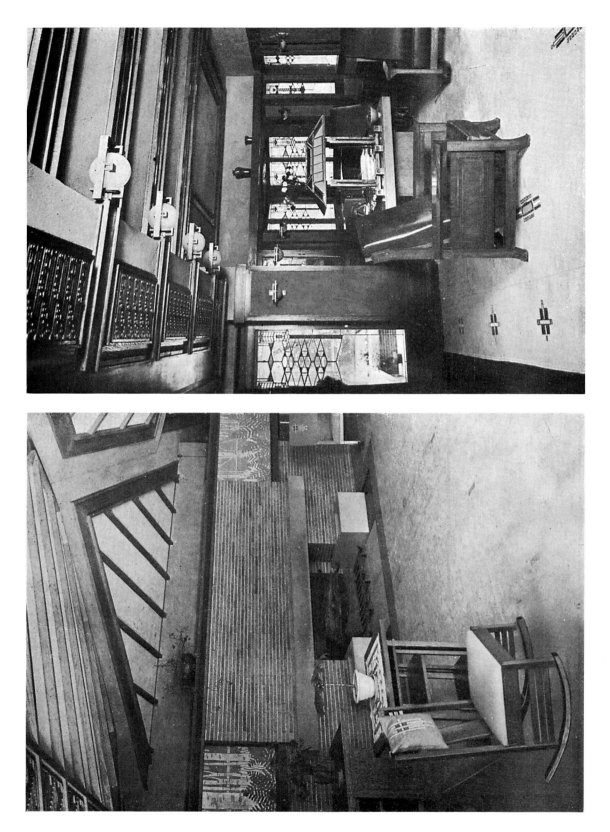

FRED C. ROBIE TOWN HOUSE, CHICAGO, ILL.: FIREPLACE (BOTTOM) AND LIVING ROOM (TOP);
THE ELECTRIC CEILING LIGHT IS FRAMED WITH WOODEN SLATS.

FRED C. ROBIE TOWN HOUSE, CHICAGO, ILL.: DINING ROOM.

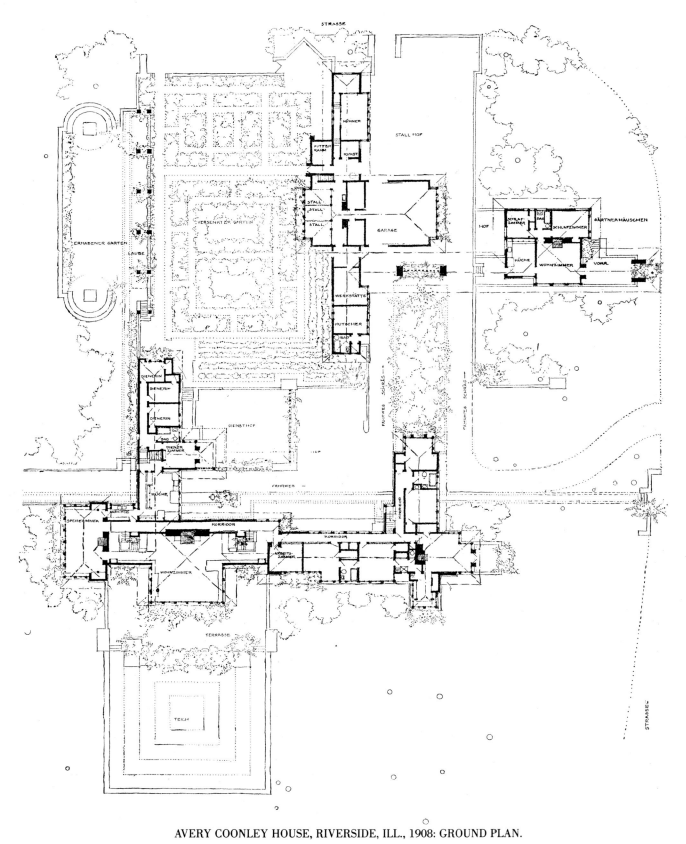

AVERY COONLEY HOUSE, RIVERSIDE, ILL., 1908: GROUND PLAN.

116

AVERY COONLEY HOUSE, RIVERSIDE, ILL.: LIVING-ROOM WING AND TERRACE.

AVERY COONLEY HOUSE, RIVERSIDE, ILL.: DINING-ROOM, LIVING-ROOM, AND
BEDROOM WINGS, CONNECTED BY GALLERIES.

AVERY COONLEY HOUSE, RIVERSIDE, ILL.: EXTERIOR DETAILS (TOP AND BOTTOM).

119

AVERY COONLEY HOUSE, RIVERSIDE, ILL.: MASTER-BEDROOM AND GUEST-ROOM WINGS.

AVERY COONLEY HOUSE, RIVERSIDE, ILL.: GALLERIES WITH SKYLIGHT, THE LIVING ROOM
IN THE MIDDLE (BOTTOM), AND DRESSING ROOM (TOP).

AVERY COONLEY HOUSE, RIVERSIDE, ILL.: DETAIL OF THE TERRACE.

AVERY COONLEY HOUSE, RIVERSIDE, ILL.: INNER (TOP) AND ENTRANCE (BOTTOM) COURTS;
WALLS WITH COLORED-TILE FACING.

123

AVERY COONLEY HOUSE, RIVERSIDE, ILL.: FIREPLACE IN THE LIVING ROOM (TOP)
AND MASTER-BEDROOM, DRESSING-ROOM, AND GUEST-ROOM WINGS (BOTTOM).

AVERY COONLEY HOUSE, RIVERSIDE, ILL.: LIVING ROOM WITH A VIEW THROUGH THE GALLERY
TOWARD THE DINING ROOM; AN ELECTRIC CEILING LIGHT IS FRAMED WITH WOODEN SLATS.

AVERY COONLEY HOUSE, RIVERSIDE, ILL.: GENERAL VIEW.

126

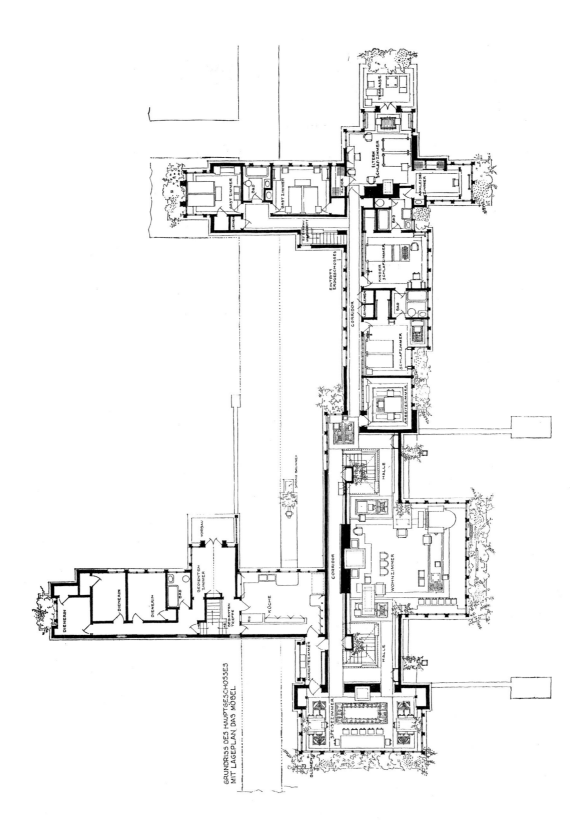

AVERY COONLEY HOUSE, RIVERSIDE, ILL.: GROUND PLAN OF THE MAIN FLOOR.

127

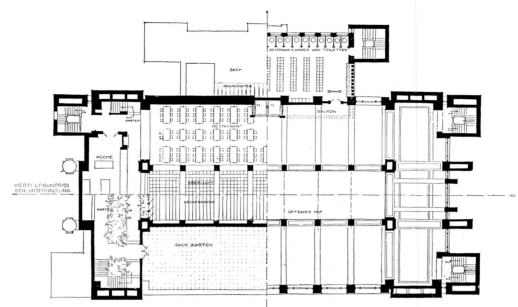

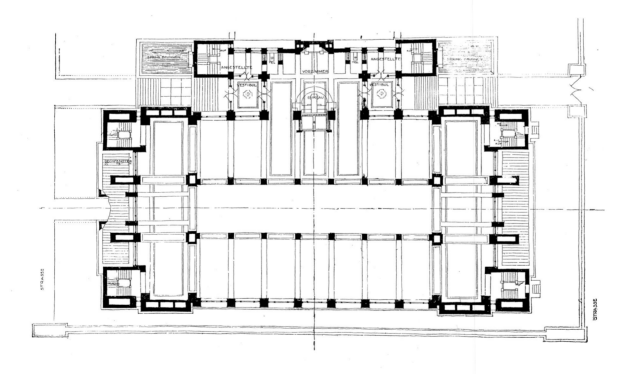

ADMINISTRATION BUILDING OF THE LARKIN FACTORIES, BUFFALO, N.Y., 1903: GROUND PLANS
(TOP AND BOTTOM).

ADMINISTRATION BUILDING OF THE LARKIN FACTORIES, BUFFALO, N.Y.

ADMINISTRATION BUILDING OF THE LARKIN FACTORIES, BUFFALO, N.Y.: CENTRAL HALL.

ADMINISTRATION BUILDING OF THE LARKIN FACTORIES, BUFFALO, N.Y.: FACADE FACING
SENECA STREET.

ADMINISTRATION BUILDING OF THE LARKIN FACTORIES, BUFFALO, N.Y.: PARTIAL VIEW OF THE
UPPER GALLERY; EXECUTED IN BRICK, MAGNESITE STONE, AND METAL.

ADMINISTRATION BUILDING OF THE LARKIN FACTORIES, BUFFALO, N.Y.: VIEW OF THE DIRECTOR'S OFFICE AND THE ADMINISTRATIVE OFFICES (TOP) AND INFORMATION DESK IN THE ENTRANCE HALL (BOTTOM); EXECUTED IN BRICK, MAGNESITE STONE, AND METAL.

ADMINISTRATION BUILDING OF THE LARKIN FACTORIES, BUFFALO, N.Y.: VIEW OF AN OFFICE;
FURNITURE OF METAL AND MAGNESITE STONE.

ADMINISTRATION BUILDING OF THE LARKIN FACTORIES, BUFFALO, N.Y.: FOUNTAIN AT THE
ENTRANCE SIDE (TOP LEFT) AND DETAILS (TOP RIGHT AND BOTTOM).

ADMINISTRATION BUILDING OF THE LARKIN FACTORIES, BUFFALO, N.Y.: VIEW OF A FLOOR DURING
WORK HOURS (TOP) AND AFTER WORK HOURS (BOTTOM).

ADMINISTRATION BUILDING OF THE LARKIN FACTORIES, BUFFALO, N.Y.: EXAMPLES OF OFFICE FURNISHINGS (TOP AND BOTTOM); DOUBLE WINDOW WITH METAL FRAME, METAL FURNITURE, AND METAL FILE CABINETS UNDER THE WINDOWS (BOTTOM).

ADMINISTRATION BUILDING OF THE LARKIN FACTORIES, BUFFALO, N.Y.: TYPICAL FLOOR LAYOUT
WITH A VIEW TOWARD THE CENTRAL HALL.

138

ADMINISTRATION BUILDING OF THE LARKIN FACTORIES, BUFFALO, N.Y.: GALLERY WITH
WRITING DESKS FOR VISITORS (BOTTOM) AND ENTRANCE TO THE EMPLOYEES' RESTROOM (TOP).

ADMINISTRATION BUILDING OF THE LARKIN FACTORIES, BUFFALO, N.Y.: FRONT ON SENECA STREET.

FRANK LLOYD WRIGHT

CHICAGO

SELECTIONS

Originally published as Number 8 of
Sonderheft der Architektur des XX Jahrhunderts
by Wasmuth, Berlin, 1911

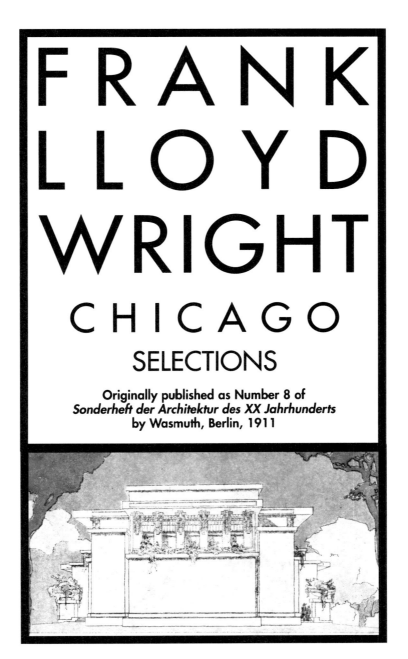

W. H. WINSLOW HOUSE, RIVER FOREST, ILL., 1893 (TOP).
OSCAR STEFFENS HOUSE, BIRCHWOOD, ILL., 1909 (BOTTOM).

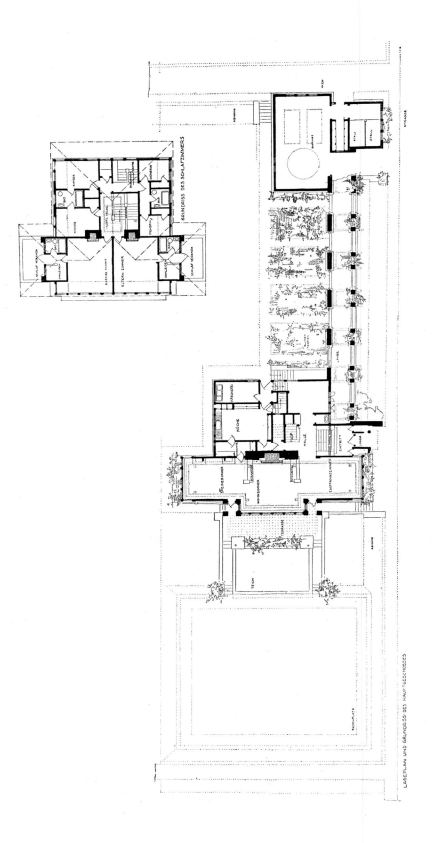

SUSAN L. DANA HOUSE, SPRINGFIELD, ILL., 1899: GROUND PLANS OF THE UPPER AND MAIN FLOORS.

F. W. LITTLE COUNTRY HOUSE, PEORIA, ILL., 1900 (TOP).
SUSAN L. DANA HOUSE, SPRINGFIELD, ILL.: SOUTH FACADE (BOTTOM).

SUSAN L. DANA HOUSE, SPRINGFIELD, ILL.

SUSAN L. DANA HOUSE, SPRINGFIELD, ILL.: SIDE ENTRANCE (TOP)
AND GALLERY INTERIOR (BOTTOM).

149

SUSAN L. DANA HOUSE, SPRINGFIELD, ILL.: ENTRANCE (BOTTOM) AND DINING ROOM (TOP).

150

D. D. MARTIN HOUSE, BUFFALO, N.Y.: CORNER OF LIVING ROOM (TOP)
AND FIREPLACE IN THE LIVING ROOM (BOTTOM).

D. D. MARTIN HOUSE, BUFFALO, N.Y.

D. D. MARTIN HOUSE, BUFFALO, N.Y.: PERGOLA (TOP) AND CONSERVATORY,
SOUTHERN VIEW (BOTTOM).

WARD W. WILLITS HOUSE, HIGHLAND PARK, ILL., 1903: SOUTH FACADE (TOP)
AND ENTRANCEWAY (BOTTOM).

ISABEL ROBERTS COUNTRY HOUSE, RIVER FOREST, ILL., 1908: LIVING ROOM WITH BALCONY ABOVE.

ISABEL ROBERTS COUNTRY HOUSE, RIVER FOREST, ILL.: ENTRANCE FACADE (TOP).
B. HARLEY BRADLEY HOUSE, KANKAKEE, ILL., 1900: LIVING ROOM (BOTTOM).

ARTHUR HEURTLEY HOUSE, OAK PARK, ILL., 1901.

ARTHUR HEURTLEY HOUSE, OAK PARK, ILL. (TOP).
J. J. WALSER HOUSE, AUSTIN, ILL., 1904 (BOTTOM).

MEYER MAY HOUSE, GRAND RAPIDS, MICH., 1909: EXTERIOR (TOP) AND LIVING ROOM (BOTTOM).

EMMA MARTIN HOUSE, OAK PARK, ILL., 1901 (TOP AND BOTTOM).

160

SPECIAL EXHIBIT OF DRAWINGS AND MODELS AT THE CHICAGO ART INSTITUTE,
CHICAGO, ILL., 1907 (TOP).
BROWNE'S BOOKSTORE, FINE ARTS BUILDING, CHICAGO, ILL., 1907 (BOTTOM).

FRANK LLOYD WRIGHT STUDIO, CHICAGO, ILL.: ENTRANCE.

FRANK LLOYD WRIGHT STUDIO, CHICAGO, ILL.: STUDY.

FRANK LLOYD WRIGHT STUDIO, CHICAGO, ILL.: ENTRANCE BEFORE ALTERATION (TOP)
AND LIBRARY (BOTTOM).

FRED C. ROBIE TOWN HOUSE, WOODLAWN AVENUE, CHICAGO, ILL., 1906: ENTRANCEWAY (TOP).
AVERY COONLEY HOUSE, RIVERSIDE, ILL., 1908: VIEW OF THE OUTSIDE
FROM THE LIVING ROOM (BOTTOM).

ADMINISTRATION BUILDING OF THE LARKIN FACTORIES, BUFFALO, N.Y., 1903:
INFORMATION DESK IN THE ENTRANCE HALL; EXECUTED IN MAGNESITE STONE AND METAL.